SPORTS INJURIES:
HOW TO PREVENT, DIAGNOSE, & TREAT

TRACK

Sports Injuries:
How to Prevent, Diagnose, & Treat

- Baseball
- Basketball
- Cheerleading
- Equestrian
- Extreme Sports
- Field
- Field Hockey
- Football
- Gymnastics
- Hockey
- Ice Skating
- Lacrosse
- Soccer
- Track
- Volleyball
- Weight Training
- Wrestling

SPORTS INJURIES: HOW TO PREVENT, DIAGNOSE, & TREAT

TRACK

CHRIS McNAB

MASON CREST PUBLISHERS
www.masoncrest.com

Mason Crest Publishers Inc.
370 Reed Road
Broomall, PA 19008
(866) MCP-BOOK (toll free)
www.masoncrest.com

2 3 4 5 6 7 8 9 10

MacNab, Chris.
Track / author, Chris MacNab.
p. cm – (Sports Injuries)
Summary: Introduces the sport of track and field and provides
information on how to prevent and treat the most common track injuries.
Includes bibliographical references and index.

ISBN 1-59084-638-9 (Hardcover : alk. paper)
1. Track and field–Juvenile literature. 2. Track and field
athletes—Wounds and Injuries—Juvenile literature. [1. Track and field.
2. Sports injuries.] I. Title. II. Series.
GV1060.55.M33 2004
796.42–dc22
2003014579

Project Editor: Michael Spilling
Design: Graham Curd
Picture Research: Natasha Jones

Printed and bound in the Hashemite Kingdom of Jordan

PICTURE CREDITS
Corbis: 6, 12, 17, 18, 20, 22, 28, 29, 36, 39, 43, 44, 47, 57, 58, 59;
©EMPICS: 11, 15, 16, 24, 26, 34, 40, 51, 54, 56;
Mary Evans Picture Library: 8, 10; **Topham Picturepoint**: 15.

FRONT COVER: All ©EMPICS, except Corbis (tl).

ILLUSTRATIONS: Courtesy of Amber Books except:
Bright Star Publishing plc: 45, 49, 53.

CONTENTS

Foreword

Sports Injuries: How to Prevent, Diagnose, and Treat is a seventeen-volume series written for young people who are interested in learning about various sports and how to participate in them safely. Each volume examines the history of the sport and the rules of play; it also acts as a guide for prevention and treatment of injuries, and includes instruction on stretching, warming up, and strength training, all of which can help players avoid the most common musculoskeletal injuries. *Sports Injuries* offers ways for readers to improve their performance and gain more enjoyment from playing sports, and young athletes will find these volumes informative and helpful in their pursuit of excellence.

Sports medicine professionals assigned to a sport that they are not familiar with can also benefit from this series. For example, a football athletic trainer may need to provide medical care for a local gymnastics meet. Although the emergency medical principles and action plan would remain the same, the athletic trainer could provide better care for the gymnasts after reading a simple overview of the principles of gymnastics in *Sports Injuries*.

Although these books offer an overview, they are not intended to be comprehensive in the recognition and management of sports injuries. The text helps the reader appreciate and gain awareness of the common injuries possible during participation in sports. Reference material and directed readings are provided for those who want to delve further into the subject.

Written in a direct and easily accessible style, *Sports Injuries* is an enjoyable series that will help young people learn about sports and sports medicine.

Susan Saliba, Ph.D., National Athletic Trainers' Association Education Council

Sprinter Michael Johnson celebrates winning a gold medal in the 400 meters (440 yd) at the 1996 Olympic Games.

History

Running began as a matter of survival: it enabled early human beings to hunt for fast prey or to escape when they themselves were hunted. As civilization spread across the globe, however, running entered into the arena of competitive sports.

The first culture to truly embrace competitive running was that of Greece. In 776 B.C.E., at the first Olympic Games, running was the only sport. The runners competed in a variety of sprint and distance events, racing in the nude around arenas that were tiny in comparison with modern stadiums.

The Olympics were discontinued in the fourth century C.E., but exploded into life again more than 1,500 years later. Many of the running events we know today were developed or refined in the nineteenth century, especially in England. Cross-country running was formed from a sport in which a group of racers, dropping pieces of paper at regular intervals, were chased across the countryside by other runners following the paper trail. It caught on quickly among England's elite schools and universities. In 1876, the first international cross-country championship was held, though it ended in farce after the foreign competitors lost their way in the unfamiliar countryside. Hurdling also developed among England's upper-class schools, and Eton College began holding hurdling competitions in 1837.

Jesse Owens is a major figure in track history. At one competition in 1935, he set three world records, despite having injured his back from falling down a flight of stairs only days before.

Running was the only event in the earliest Olympics in Greece. The athletes competed barefooted and must have had very durable feet and limbs.

As the nineteenth century progressed, more running events were added to the British sporting calendar. In 1850, Exeter College held the world's first track-and-field competition using many of the athletics events we know today, including distance sprints such as the 400 meters (440 yd). In the same year, Oxford University introduced the steeplechase event. New distances were added to established sports, such as the 110 meters (120 yd) and 400 meters (440 yd) for the hurdles in 1864.

By the second half of the nineteenth century, competitive running had spread across Europe and into the United States. In 1896, the Olympic Games were roused from their long sleep. Athens, the capital city of Greece, was chosen to host the games. Running events were held both inside and outside the stadium. Track events, such as the 100 meters (110 yd) sprint and the 1,500 meters (1,640 yd) distance run, were performed on the circular Olympic track, while the marathon event took the runners 25 miles (40 km) around the Greek capital.

MODERN TRACK EVENTS

In men's athletics, the full range of men's running events had entered the Olympics by 1920. It took a lot longer for the women's events. For example, men were running the 10,000 meters (10,940 yd) race in 1912, but it was not until 1988 that the same event was run by women.

Today's athletic track events are separated into eight basic categories. Some, such as the 100 meters sprint, are performed on an athletics track, while others, like the cross-country and marathon, take place in the countryside and on urban roads. The eight categories of running events are as follows:

Sprint

Modern sprinting has three distances: 100 meters (110 yd), 200 meters (220 yd), and 400 meters (440 yd). The 100 meters is run in fixed lanes along a straight track,

Top athletes battle for position in the women's 100 meters (110 yd) hurdles event in the Sydney (Australia) Olympics in 2000. Professionals only take about four strides between each hurdle.

RELAY RACE

In the late 1800s in the United States, teams of city firefighters raced each other, passing a red pennant to the next racer in line about every 275 yards (250 m). The game became a sport in the 1880s, and the first official relay competition took place in 1893. Although relay was not a feature of the revived Olympics in 1896, the men's 4 x 100 meters and 4 x 400 meters relay were run in the 1912 Stockholm Olympics. The women's 4 x 100 meters entered the Olympics in 1928 and the 4 x 400 meters only in 1972. With the introduction of this latter event, competitive track events had reached the form that we know today.

A fast transfer is the key to a successful relay team in competitive racing.

and today's athletes cover about 11 yards (10 m) every second. The 200 meters, despite the increased distance, is run at a similar speed—a top international sprinter can reach 25 miles per hour (40 km/h) in the 200 meters and finish within twenty seconds. The biggest tactical difference is that the sprinter has to negotiate a bend during the sprint. The 400 meters involves two bends, and the greatest speed of the race is usually attained during the last straight 100 meters.

Hurdles

There are three categories of hurdles—100 m, 110 m (120 yd), and 400 m—and ten hurdles in each race. The runner is not penalized for knocking down hurdles unless the action is deliberate or the foot goes under the hurdle bar. Today's hurdles are 3 ft 6 in (106 cm) high for men and 2 ft 9 in (84 cm) high for women.

Relay

Olympic relay has two distances: 4 x 100 m and 4 x 400 m. The four runners have specific zones in which they must pass over the hollow wooden or plastic baton. These zones are 32 ft (10 m) on either side of the next runner's start line. Apart from the two Olympic distances, other relay distances in non-Olympic competitions include the 3,200 m (3,500 yd) and 6,000 m (6,560 yd).

Middle distance

Middle-distance track events refer to the 800 m (875 yd), 1,000 m (1,094 yd), and 1,500 m (1,640 yd) distances. In both races, the runners do not have to stay in dedicated lanes. The result is a dense group of runners, each using his or her own tactics to attempt victory. Some will attempt to lead from the front the whole way around, while others will hang back in preparation for a final burst of speed.

Steeplechase

Steeplechase is a 3,000-meter (3,280-yd) race featuring hurdles and water jumps. The standard configuration is twenty-eight non-collapsible hurdles, each 3 ft (91 cm) high, and seven water jumps, each preceded by a hurdle. The water jump is 27 in (70 cm) deep at its deepest point beneath the hurdle, and 12 ft (3.66 m) long.

Long-distance runs

Excluding marathon and cross-country, the main long-distance track events are the 5,000 meters (5,470 yd) and the 10,000 meters (10,940 yd). These races test stamina and endurance, but they also require tactical running—applying speed at the right times and hanging back occasionally to conserve energy.

Cross-country

Cross-country is run over distances of 2½, 5, and 7½ miles (4, 8, and 12 km), although 5 miles is for women only. Cross-country runners handle all types of terrain and climates, and the body takes a real hammering. The runs vary widely in terms of the numbers of competitors, from fewer than fifty up to many thousands.

Marathon

The marathon was set at a distance of 26 miles (42 km) in 1908. Major marathon events are held in cities throughout the world, including Boston and London, and can draw in more than 25,000 competitors.

GREAT MODERN RUNNERS

Today's professional athletes have achieved standards unimaginable at the time of the first Olympics. Take sprinting, for example: at the end of the nineteenth

Steve Holman (U.S.A.) runs in the Men's 1,500 meters (1,640 yd) semi-final at the Sixth IAAF World Championships in Athens, 1997.

century, Thomas Burke of United States set a time of 12 seconds for the 100-meters dash. Jump forward just over 100 years and Maurice Greene, also of United States, set a new world record of 9.79 seconds for the same distance.

These remarkable improvements in performance are, in part, the results of better diet, improved understanding of **physiology**, more advanced training equipment and techniques, and better running shoes. But we cannot take away from the genuine achievements of today's athletes.

The United States has been especially dominant in the world of sprinting. Since 1960, almost all sprint world records have been set by U.S. athletes. Names include Jim Hines; Calvin Smith; Florence Griffith-Joyner, whose world record for the 200 meters still stands; and the legendary Carl Lewis, who achieved seventeen international gold medals during his career and a personal best in the 100 meters of 9.86 seconds. In the 200 meters and 400 meters, Michael Johnson was another U.S. powerhouse. His crowning glory came in the 1996 Olympics in Atlanta. There, he set a world record for the 200 meters of 19.32 seconds. Johnson also won the 400 meters in 43.49 seconds.

In other track events besides sprinting, the United States has not been as powerful. In middle- and long-distance runs, nations such as Great Britain, Russia, Kenya,

Ethiopia, Italy, China, and Czechoslovakia have all put winners on the medals podium. Kenyan athletes held on to the world records in the steeplechase for a remarkable twenty-three years—Moses Kitanui was the first runner to complete the 3,000 meters steeplechase in under eight minutes. In 2001, Kenya lost the world record to Brahim Boulami from Morocco. He ran 3,000 meters in a time of 7:55:28 in Brussels, Belgium. Ethiopia has fielded the phenomenal runner Haile Gebrselassie, who currently holds the world records in the 5,000 and 10,000 meters.

Because the standards of world records today are so high, fewer are being broken. U.S. athletes in history have some important accolades, however. In 1936, African-American athlete Jesse Owens smashed Hitler's theory of white supremacy when he set six world records in one day, and took four gold medals in the Berlin Olympics. In World Championship events, Michael Johnson has the record for the most gold medals—nine in total. Gail Devers of the United States holds the women's version of the same title, having won five gold medals between 1993 and 1997. Yet standards of athletic training in the United States are so high that even such lofty records are not safe.

Gail Devers (U.S.A.) battled chronic illness to become a world record holder and twice an Olympic 100 meters (110 yd) sprint gold medalist.

RACEWALKING

Racewalking is a distinctive event within track and field. The athletes have to walk at speed over long distances. They propel themselves using an awkward and physically demanding technique that uses the whole body, especially the arms and hips. An expert walker can achieve speeds of 9 miles per hour (15 km/h) and maintain it for hours. At the end of the twentieth century, the world records for 20-km (12-mile) speed walks stood at less than eighty minutes. The current distances for speed walking are 10 km (6 miles), 20 km (12 miles), and 50 km (31 miles).

Race walkers have to maintain a pace which is two or three times that of normal walking. At no point must both feet leave the ground — this would mean that they are, in effect, running and are subject to disqualification from the race.

Mental Preparation

Ignoring mental preparation is an ideal way to underperform in athletics. The world's best runners now often employ sports psychologists to give them the mental edge in training and competition.

There are several factors that distinguish medal-winning athletes from those who never achieve their full potential. One of the most important is a positive frame of mind. Professional sportspeople are now taught techniques of Positive Mental Attitude (**P.M.A.**) to improve their running performance. How does this work? There are two elements to P.M.A. First, you must take control of your inner voice, that part of your brain which offers a running commentary on how you feel and think. Say only positive things to yourself when you think about your running. Instead of "I'll never win this event," tell yourself "I can become a top competitor in this event." Instead of "That person is much better than me," tell yourself "I will learn everything I can from them to improve my performance." When you catch yourself thinking negative thoughts, immediately follow them with positive contradictions. Repeat this pattern often enough and you will find that P.M.A. becomes a habit. The result is that you will not be so easily discouraged by difficulty and problems. For complex medical reasons, being happier also creates more physical energy to use on the track.

The second element of P.M.A. involves your imagination. Set time aside for mental training, creating positive visual pictures of your performance in running events.

An athlete readies himself for a sprint. He must not move until the gun sounds. A common cause of disqualification is the athlete anticipating the gun and setting off too early.

The key is to imagine everything in detail. For example, see yourself in the 1500 meters pushing out ahead of the pack toward the finish line; hear the noise of the crowds cheering; and feel your running shoes hitting the track and the sensation of your deep breathing. Mentally rehearse your technique until it is perfect. Also picture your tactics. In the 1,500 meters a common tactic is to run close behind another competitor to reduce wind resistance. Then, as you approach the finish line, you use the energy you have saved to sprint out from behind the other runner and pass ahead to cross the finish line. Practice this tactic in your imagination, and visualize the success it brings you. Also, be creative. Imagine you are a racehorse, using your great muscular advantage to pass the other merely human competitors.

Victory can be a mixed blessing. Let it give you more confidence, but avoid becoming overconfident and not training as hard. Remember, someone else is always after your title.

The point to these thoughts—known technically as **visualization**—is that they have a real impact on physical performance. Research has shown that athletes who practice visualization produce better times than those who do not.

The final part of P.M.A. includes positive body posture. To see what this means, try a physical experiment. Stand up straight, pull back your shoulders, and lift up your chin. Put a big smile on your face, even if it feels artificial. Go for a brisk ten-minute walk, swinging your arms and filling your lungs with air. Use all your senses to enjoy the world around you.

As you do this, you will probably begin to feel more energetic, lively, and intelligent, and less prone to depression and worry. The fact is, our thoughts often follow what our bodies are doing, rather than the other way around. By acting happy and confident, we actually become happy and confident. You can use this to help your track performance.

Act like you are a winning runner. Stand up tall and proud, and imitate the confident athletic behavior of successful professional athletes. Strange as it may sound, by acting as if you are going to win a race, you will actually increase the likelihood of doing so.

KEEPING A RECORD

By filling in a log after every training session, you will gain detailed insight into how you are developing and what needs to be changed. The log can also help prevent injuries. If, for example, you look back over your log and discover **Achilles tendon** problems shortly after practicing sprint starts, then you can either alter your start technique or refrain from practicing starts while the injury heals. In addition to training entries, make special entries for competitions. Note the same information as above, but also enter some details about how you felt at

CHECKING YOUR PROGRESS

A major part of your mental training should be keeping track of your progress. Keep an account of your times, competition performance, and medals to help you see how far you have come, and also to identify those areas which need

Advancing up the various levels of competition usually means meeting the qualifying times set by the U.S.A. Track and Field organization and beating those times in competition.

more work. The best way of keeping track is through a training log. The training log is a notebook or computer database for recording day-to-day details about your athletic training. The following are the types of information you want to include in each entry:

- date;
- weather;
- type of run;
- type of training footwear worn;
- times achieved;

- warm-up techniques used;
- cool-down techniques used;
- special training techniques;
- notes about performance;
- injuries.

the competition and how you prepared for it. Again, you may find a revealing insight into what is controlling your performance.

COMPETITIONS

Your mental training matters more than ever in competitions. Many fine athletes have been defeated in races because a lack of confidence spoils their physical ability. Competitions are undoubtedly nerve-wracking events. There are several things you can do, however, to help you harness your nervousness so that instead of weakening your body, it makes you run faster:

1. Pack up everything you need for the race before you go to bed. This means you will probably sleep better and also have a more restful morning on the day of the race.

2. Eat properly throughout the day. Do not eat large, meaty meals because these will make you feel sluggish and lacking in energy, particularly if your race is in the afternoon, following lunch. Also, make sure you have a good, healthy breakfast: cereal, toast, orange juice, and fruit. Breakfast is the most important meal of the day because your brain needs it for energy throughout the morning.

3. Warm up properly once you get to the place where the race is to be held. Not only will this loosen up your body and prepare it for the race, but it will also help you focus your mind on what you need to do.

4. Psych yourself up. Focus one hundred percent on the race ahead of you. Find a place by yourself, where you can shut out other concerns and concentrate on the techniques needed to win. If you find it helps, play your favorite music on portable headphones. Also, do not be intimidated by other competitors. Concentrate solely on getting from the starting line to the finish line in the fastest possible time, and forget the behavior of others.

5. Learn from your defeats. Defeats are not easy to accept, but you must learn to

Sprinters in the 100 meters (110 yd) race accelerate for the first two-thirds of the race, achieving their maximum speed around 60 meters (196 ft).

cope with them if you are going to improve. Steve Scott, the U.S. record holder in the 1-mile (1.6-km) run, gives the following advice for coping with disappointment: "I give myself an hour, two hours tops, to be upset or angry about a bad race. I think about what went wrong and why it might have gone wrong, but I don't beat myself up about it."

Like Steve, do not give yourself very long for feeling depression or regret. Quickly concentrate on why the race was a problem, and write down in your training log anything that occurs to you. Return to your training with renewed enthusiasm, determined to conquer your problems and smash your times in the next race in which you compete.

TACTICS FOR SPRINT RACING

The U.S.A. Track and Field organization recommends the following tactics for effective sprint racing:

1. Move immediately into the set position on the starter's command. The gun may be quick.

2. Start only at the gun.

3. Work on a quick, consistent reaction, but do not seek an advantage by trying to predict the starter's rhythm of commands. In training, vary the rhythm so that you get used to spending different times in the set position.

4. Establish a race pattern before competing. Competition is no place to learn.

5. Be prepared to race in any of the lanes, and for your main competition to be beside you or several lanes away.

6. Check that the blocks are set to your specifications and securely anchored.

7. Know where the finish line is—and always run through it! Dip at the line only when absolutely necessary.

8. Never treat preliminary rounds of competition lightly. Know the time or place required to qualify for the next round.

9. Systematically warm up and cool down before and after every race.

10. Know the shoe requirements at every track. Be prepared with a wrench and extra spikes.

(*Source: USATF Level 1 Curriculum*)

Physical Preparation to Prevent Injury

A proper warm-up is integral to safe running. Many amateur runners—particularly distance runners—neglect the warm-up stage of training. They expose themselves to pulled muscles and strained joints.

While it is certainly true that a runner requires less overall body flexibility than, say, a gymnast, this is missing the point. A warm-up is not about achieving unusual flexibility, but about making sure that your muscles are not damaged by their normal range of movement. Cold muscles have far less flexibility than warm muscles and are more liable to be strained if put under sudden intense exercise. When a person is running, many muscle groups and other body tissues are working hard. In the legs alone, the Achilles tendon, calf muscles, **hamstrings**, **quadriceps**, ankle and foot **flexors**, **sartorius muscles** of the upper thighs, and the **gluteus maximus** muscles of the buttocks are all stretching and flexing in rapid motion. Warming up means that the body is made ready to face these demands.

WARM-UP ROUTINE FOR RUNNERS

A complete warm-up consists of two elements: light exercise to raise the temperature of the body, and stretching exercises to make muscles more flexible.

Runners should begin a training session with a comprehensive warm up, which should include stretching their hamstring, calf, and hip flexor muscles.

A stretching session before training should last for ten to fifteen minutes, though you may need to do one or two refresher stretches as you cool off between events.

Here we will look at a sequence of exercises that are specifically designed to meet the needs of runners.

The first stage of the warm-up is to gently increase muscle temperature, heartbeat, and breathing through light exercise. To do this, jog very gently on the spot for about five minutes. Slowly raise the knees higher as you go along, but do not let the thighs rise to an angle of more than 45° to the ground. Shake your arms loosely by your sides occasionally to relax your shoulder and arm muscles. If you get bored with running, you can switch to another exercise such as **star jumps**. Whatever you do, do not push yourself to intense exercise—that will come later in training.

Finish the initial stage of the warm-up by hip- and shoulder-loosening exercises. For the hips, stand with your feet shoulder-width apart and your hands on your hips. Circle the hips in one direction, as if spinning an imaginary Hula-Hoop, and make circles that are as large as possible. Do this about ten times in one direction. Then reverse, for ten times in the other direction.

To warm up the shoulders, make large circles forward with the arms, bringing your hands together in front of you and brushing the hips at the bottom of the swing. Do this in one direction ten times, then reverse.

Once you have completed these exercises, you are ready to move on to the next stage, which is stretching.

FLEXIBILITY TRAINING

Flexible runners have better stride efficiency than inflexible runners. This means that they will be able to achieve a greater average length or stride, and have more power throughout the stride—in short, they are faster. They are also less likely to suffer from overuse injuries or sprains and strains.

Here we will look at some of the best stretches for improving lower-limb and hip flexibility in preparation for running events. Before we do so, there are a few general rules about making stretching efficient and safe.

Breathe out when sinking down into any stretch. Releasing the breath results in muscles relaxing, and relaxed muscles are capable of stretching farther than tense muscles.

To stretch the groin, place the soles of your feet together, push the knees slowly downward to the maximum stretch and hold for about ten seconds.

First, perform all stretches slowly and smoothly. Avoid any jerking or bouncing movements because these are more likely to result in strained muscles. Breathe deeply throughout any stretch—muscles need oxygen when they are under exertion. Try to relax while stretching. Do not tense the muscles, but imagine them softening. If you experience pain or burning sensations, stop stretching immediately.

Ankle stretch

Sitting down, put the left ankle on top of the right knee. Hold the raised ankle with your left hand, and take hold of the toes and the ball of the foot with your right hand. Using your right hand, circle the foot around in one direction in large circles. Repeat about ten times, then reverse and repeat with the other foot.

Achilles tendon stretch

Lie on your back with both knees bent and feet flat on the floor. Straighten one leg up into the air and hold it with both hands on the calf muscle. Pull your leg gently toward your face until it is at maximum stretch. Then flex the raised foot slowly backward and forward about ten times, working the Achilles tendon.

Lower-leg stretch

Sit on the floor with both legs straight out in front of you. Draw one leg in so that the sole of the foot sits against the inner thigh of the opposite leg. Sit up straight and breathe in deeply, then exhale slowly and bend forward from the hips and waist over the extended leg until you can grip your foot. Slowly pull on the toes so that the heel lifts slightly off the floor. You should feel a deep stretch along the back of the leg and knee. Lower the heel to the floor and sit up slowly. Then reverse legs and repeat the exercise.

Note: if you are not flexible enough to reach your foot, place a folded towel or belt over the toes and hold onto this instead.

Quadriceps stretch

Stand up straight, resting one hand against a wall for stability. Lift your left leg behind you and grasp the top of the foot with your left hand, then pull the heel up toward your buttocks. You should feel the stretch along the front of the thigh and the knee. Hold the position for about thirty seconds, then let go of the foot and return it to the floor. Repeat for your right leg.

Groin stretch

Sit on the floor and draw your feet into the groin, pressing the soles of the feet together so that the knees fall outward. Grasp your ankles with your hands, and use your elbows to push down on the knees. This stretch is concentrated along the inside of the groin. Hold the stretch for about twenty seconds, then gently release the pressure on your knees and bring them up to the center.

The quadriceps stretch can be performed leaning against a wall for support. Keep the knees close together to maximize the stretch and make the supporting leg straight.

Hip stretch

Stand with your feet one shoulder-width apart. Place your hands on your hips. Step forward with one leg into a deep single-knee bend—the thigh of your bent leg should be at an angle of 90° to the shin. In this position, exhale, then sink the hip on the side of the rear leg down toward the floor. Hold the hip stretch for about ten seconds, then repeat the stretch on the other side.

This sequence of stretches should be performed about three times a week and directly before running, to ensure that your lower limbs are ready for exercise. Note, however, that the legs and hips are not the only parts of the body we should stretch before running. The back is another particularly important area. During a run, it has to undergo constant impact and flexing actions, so it needs to be prepared. A simple back stretch follows:

Back stretch

Stand with your feet shoulder-width apart. Bend straight forward from the waist and lower your torso as far as it will go, keeping your back straight. Holding the legs and gently pulling on them will help you to go down farther. Hold the stretch for about ten seconds, then move your body upright again. Place your hands against your lower back and stretch your upper body backward, looking up at the ceiling as you do. Hold for ten seconds, then release. This stretch also works the **abdominals** and hips.

A thorough warm-up and stretch will prepare your body for a vigorous run. You may find that you cool off between your warm-up and an event—something which commonly happens during competitions. If so, repeat the warm-up for safety.

WEIGHT TRAINING FOR RUNNERS

Weight training builds up the muscles of the legs, hips, back, abdomen, arms, and shoulders, giving a runner greater speed and endurance. For those under the age of eighteen, there are several important rules to note:

- Get expert instruction in the correct use of freeweights and weight machines. Poor technique is a primary cause of injury. When learning a new exercise, practice lifting no weight at all until you can demonstrate proper technique.

- Do not attempt to lift extremely heavy weights. These may build up your muscle bulk so much that the muscles lose their power to expand and contract quickly, which could make you a slower runner.

- Do not weight-train more than three times a week, and keep training sessions under forty-five minutes.

- Breathe deeply throughout any weightlifting exercise. Breathe out as you push, pull, or lift the weight, and breathe in as you move it to its starting position. Never lift weights with fast, jerky movements.

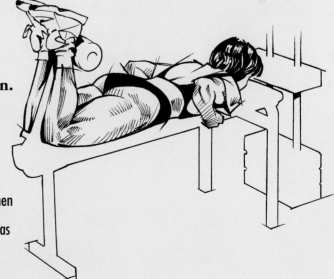

Leg curls can be used both to strengthen the calf muscles and hamstrings, and as a light rehabilitation exercise.

Footwear

Good footwear is extremely important for a runner. Without a properly-fitted shoe, designed to meet the demands of the particular event, the athlete is exposed to wear-and-tear injuries in the feet, legs, hips, and back.

Finding the right type of shoe is not just a case of choosing one designed for your particular sport. You must also select shoes for your particular foot behavior.

There are basically three classifications of foot behavior during running: normal **pronation**, **overpronation**, and **underpronation**. These terms sound very technical, but they are relatively easy to understand.

NORMAL PRONATION

When a foot strikes the floor in events other than sprinting, the heel impacts on the floor first, then the foot rolls along the length of the sole to the toe. Pronation refers to the way in which the arch of your foot also rolls slightly toward the inside as it absorbs the pressure of your step. Someone with normal pronation has only a slight inward roll, which causes no significant problems.

OVERPRONATION

Overpronation means that the foot rolls inward to an excessive degree. The arch of the foot collapses too much in an attempt to withstand the pressure of impact.

Sandra Glover (U.S.A.) prepares herself for the 400 m. (440 yd.) hurdles event. Hurdler's shoes are like those worn by sprinters, with a short section of spikes at the front, but have a reinforced heel to withstand landings.

This is a problem because more of the impact is then channeled upward into the joints of the ankles, knees, and hips.

UNDERPRONATION

Someone who underpronates has no, or extremely little, inward foot roll. This can be as much of a problem as overpronation. Without a certain amount of inward roll, more shock is channeled into the leg. Underpronation can even become a rare problem called **supination**, when the foot actually rolls along the outer edge, causing injuries in feet, ankles, and knees.

When trying on sports shoes, put them through the full range of movement that they will experience in your event. They should be firm-fitting and not slip at any point.

Take a close look at a pair of your well-worn shoes. Check the sole of one shoe. More wear on the inside means you are overpronating. If the shoe is worn evenly from instep to toe, it means that you have normal pronation. Excessive wear on the outside edge of the shoe indicates underpronation.

CHOOSING THE RIGHT SHOE

Shoe technology is a large subject, but there are some basic details you should know. There are roughly five types of running shoe:

Cushioned shoe

Designed for people with normal pronation, this has plenty of foam cushioning in the **midsole**, a region between the sole of the shoe and the **upper**.

Motion-control shoe

This includes features designed to correct overpronation. A typical feature is a medial post—a harder piece of midsole material on the inside of the shoe to support the foot arch.

Stability shoe

Designed for people without pronation problems, but providing good support to the arch of the foot, this shoe is useful for physically heavy runners or when running over rough ground.

Racing shoe/lightweight training shoe

A light and very flexible shoe used for sprinting or other fast runs. It does not generally have as much support as the other types of footwear.

CARING FOR SPORTS FOOTWEAR

Once you have bought running shoes, look after them:

- Do not wear them for anything other than training or competing.
- Keep them clean, using professional shoe cleaning products.
- Do not allow dirt to build up in the treads of the soles. Clean the dirt out with a stiff brush.
- Once the soles are worn, it is time to replace the shoe. Running with worn shoes means that you do not have the full level of foot protection, so wear-and-tear injuries are far more likely. For distance runners, many athletes recommend changing of shoes about every 400–500 miles (640–800 km).

Trail shoe

Used for cross-country running, this shoe has a sole with advanced tread features for extra grip and, usually, a lot of support around the ankle to prevent twisting the foot on uneven ground.

Choosing the right shoe depends on which events you run, and also what type of support your feet need. The important point about choosing the correct shoes is to get the right advice when buying. Choose your shoes in close consultation with a professional assistant in a good sports store or through your athletic team.

Former Olympic and World 1500-meters (1640 yd) champion Sebastian Coe puts on his running shoes before a race. Wear running shoes with a proper pair of running socks. The socks affect the fit of shoes, so also wear your running socks when trying on new footwear.

Common Injuries and Their Treatment

As you would expect, the vast majority of running injuries are concentrated in the legs. Every time a foot strikes the floor during a sprint or distance run, tons of pressure are sent up the leg.

It is little wonder that many professional track athletes succumb to stress injuries through overuse. Before we look at various running injuries, we will first consider a set of common treatment techniques. Many injuries do not need professional treatment—mainly non-serious sprains and strains—and these may be treated in three stages. The first of these stages may be remembered by the acronym **P.R.I.C.E.**, which stands for Protection, Rest, Ice, Compression, and Elevation:

PROTECTION

Stop exercising immediately, and move to a place or position where you can take pressure off the injured area.

Rest

Give the injured area complete rest for at least a week. Restrict other activities and sports that affect the injury, including everyday walking.

The United States' Suzy Favor Hamilton (no. 3348) is ranked among the world's best middle-distance runners. She has suffered a lot of injuries and recommends avoiding concrete running surfaces.

Ice

Reduce any swelling around the injury by applying ice packs about two or three times a day, for no longer than twenty minutes each time. If there is no swelling, however, you may find it more beneficial to apply heat treatments after the first few days. Heat-generating ointments are available from sports stores and drug stores, and are useful for reducing pain in muscle strains. Do not use heat treatments on swelling or swollen areas.

Compression

Wrap the injury firmly in a bandage or athletic tape. Even better, use a professional compression bandage. The pressure around the injury reduces swelling, and also protects the joint or muscle against further damage.

Elevation

Elevate an injured limb on a surface such as a chair or table that is well-padded with cushions. If the leg is injured, try to raise it higher than the hips. Elevation reduces the amount of blood flowing into a limb, and so helps reduce swelling.

Following the P.R.I.C.E. procedure alone may enable you to return to training after about a week and is ideal for sprained ankles, a common running injury. If, however, the injured muscle or joint is pain-free but stiff or weak after this time, there are two more treatments that may be tried. First are range of motion (**R.O.M.**) exercises. These are light stretching and flexibility exercises, meant to restore the full range of movement to the joint or limb. The stretches are gentle, but should explore movement in every direction that was possible before the accident. The goal is to achieve full mobility without any stiffness or pain.

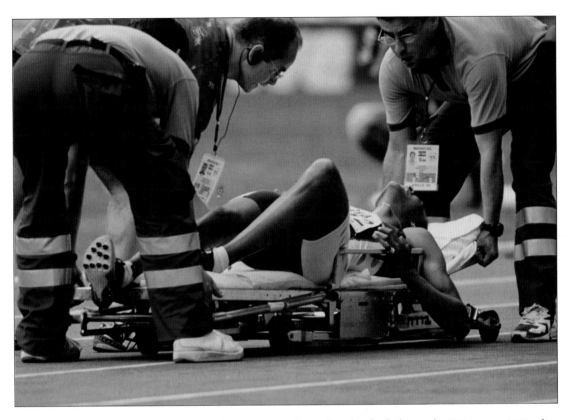

U.S. athlete Marion Jones is put on a stretcher, in agony, after pulling her back during the 100 meters (110 yd) at the 1999 World Championships. Sprinting puts extreme forces on the lower back.

Once you have full, pain-free R.O.M., you need to strengthen the injured joint or muscle. Light weight training is a good way of achieving this. Barbell squats, leg extensions, legs presses, leg curls, and hip adduction are excellent rehabilitation exercises for the lower limbs—ask your coach or at your local gym for details. Do not load the bar or weight machine with heavy weights. Practice first lifting weights of only 1–2 pounds (0.5–1 kg) until you can perform the technique perfectly for at least eight repetitions without struggling. Add more weight in 1–3 pounds (0.5–1.5 kg) increments. Such gentle weight training over a period of about seven days should get your injured joint or muscle back into condition.

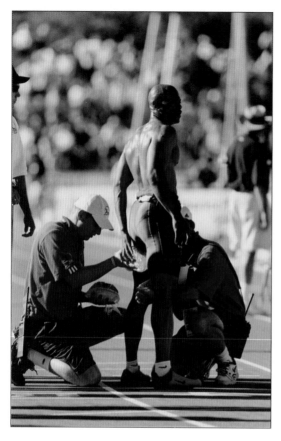

A coach ices U.S. runner Maurice Greene's hamstring muscle during a training session.

At any stage during rehabilitation, stop exercising if the pain returns, or you experience any burning sensations in the joint or muscle. Remember, too, that self-treatment is an option only for simple and identifiable injuries. If you are not sure what is wrong, are experiencing significant pain consult a doctor immediately.

ACHILLES TENDON INJURIES

The Achilles tendon is the prominent tendon at the back of the heel, which joins the heel to the muscles of the lower leg. Runners tend to injure it in two ways. First is Achilles tendonitis, where the Achilles tendon suffers from gradual wear and tear, producing a steady buildup of pain and stiffness at the back of the heel. Running up hills and wearing running shoes with very stiff soles or very deep, soft heels are major causes of Achilles tendonitis because these can lead to excessive stretching of the tendon.

More serious than tendonitis is a complete rupture. The cause of a ruptured Achilles tendon may be a twisted ankle, but is more commonly associated with excessive stretching exercises. A ruptured tendon will be agonizing and the ankle will be almost immobile, leaving you in no doubt that you must consult a doctor.

Treating Achilles tendonitis may be a simple matter of reducing your training commitments. Avoid long-distance runs and strenuous hills, and make sure that you have at least three days each week with no exercise. Apply ice packs to reduce pain and swelling. During rehabilitation, it is best to avoid putting the Achilles tendon through stretching exercises. Instead, do gentle circling of the foot and ankle. Strengthen the tendon by gradually returning to running.

A ruptured tendon is usually treated by surgery, after which you may be in a cast for twelve weeks and possibly have **physical therapy** for up to one year. You cannot treat a ruptured tendon yourself, and you should always follow the guidance of a qualified doctor.

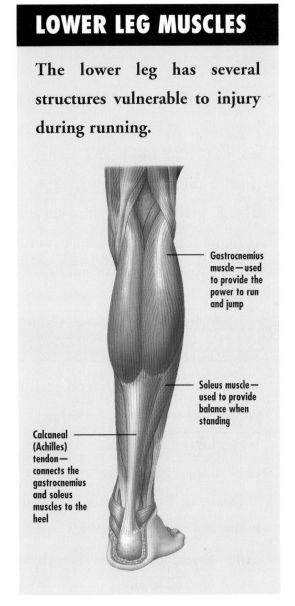

LOWER LEG MUSCLES

The lower leg has several structures vulnerable to injury during running.

Gastrocnemius muscle—used to provide the power to run and jump

Soleus muscle—used to provide balance when standing

Calcaneal (Achilles) tendon—connects the gastrocnemius and soleus muscles to the heel

KNEE INJURIES

The knee is a complicated joint that joins the **tibia** bone of the lower leg and the **femur** bone of the thigh, and it includes many working parts. The symptoms of knee damage in runners usually include:

- pain down the side or front of the knee. Depending on the condition, the pain often worsens with exercise, particularly when running or walking down hills;
- stiffness in the joint;
- pain following periods of sitting with the knees bent.

The P.R.I.C.E., R.O.M., and strengthening sequence of treatment usually suffices to treat a minor knee injury. You may benefit, however, from reducing the P.R.I.C.E. period or even skipping it altogether. Studies into knee rehabilitation have found that an injured knee joint tends to benefit from movement and light exercise. Sitting on a high chair or table, practice moving the lower leg backward

STITCH

Stitch is a nonserious complaint experienced by almost all distance runners at some time or other. It is a familiar pain felt just under the ribs during exertion. The causes of stitch range from poorly conditioned abdominal muscles to eating too close to training.

Treat stitch by first slackening off the pace of your running and breathing very deeply. Pull breaths right down to your stomach, then expel them fully. Also breathe rhythmically without holding your breath at any point.

If these measures fail to relieve the pain, stop running but maintain the breathing. The stitch should pass fairly quickly once you do this. To prevent stitch in the future, do abdominal exercises such as crunches and sit-ups to condition your stomach muscles and diaphragm.

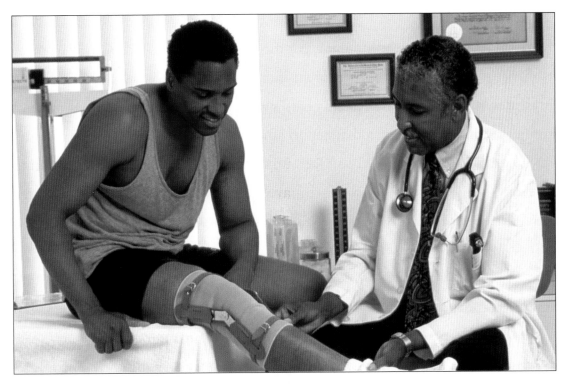

A brace provides support to an injured joint or muscle while it heals. Braces can be rigid or "functional" (may allow a limited range of joint movement), and are only fitted by doctors.

and forward through its full range of movement to reintroduce mobility and strength. For additional support, you can put a physical therapy ball under the foot to take pressure off the knee. Further strengthening is available through lower-limb weight-training exercises, but only if you experience no significant pain. Try the exercises without weights before proceeding.

Return to running gently. For the first few weeks, try to avoid running continuously around track bends—these put the knee under more pressure. Consult a doctor if the pain in the knee increases or knee flexibility decreases at any time during rehabilitation. Also consult a doctor if the joint feels unstable or its movement is rough.

SHIN SPLINTS

Shin splints is a non-technical name for medial tibial stress syndrome. It refers to pain that occurs in the front or side of the shin, caused by injury to the bone, muscles, or **ligaments** in the area as a result of hard sporting activity. Shin splints are a classic runner's injury. They tend to happen to athletes who are overtraining or running on hard tracks or other hard surfaces. In fact, if you suddenly change running surfaces—as in moving from cross-country to track—increase your time on the new surface gradually in order to reduce the risk of shin splints. This injury also

OVERUSE INJURIES

An overuse, or chronic, injury is caused by repeating the same action many times. This is not as serious as an acute injury, but any chronic problem may become worse if not acknowledged early on, so runners should seek medical advice and treatment. Overuse injuries have both mental and physical symptoms:

- unusual tiredness or fatigue
- feeling very emotional, particularly depressed, anxious, or stressed
- a lack of appetite
- an inability to sleep at night
- muscle soreness and cramps
- stiff, painful, or unstable joints
- problems getting parts of the body comfortable in bed at night
- painful tendons
- pain that shows no improvement for more than three days

strikes runners with over- or underpronation, so make sure that you have the correct shoes fitted for your feet and for the running surface. Replace worn shoes.

The symptoms of shin splints typically include:

- pain in the shin area that grows worse with activity and lets up with rest;
- some swelling over the shin area;
- pain in the shin when the foot is flexed.

Virtually the only treatment for shin splints is rest. Stop training immediately and let the injury heal naturally, which could take up to four months in severe cases. Use the P.R.I.C.E. procedure to control any swelling, and take painkillers to control the pain. R.O.M. and strengthening exercises are of limited value for shin splints and should not be attempted until there is no pain in the shin when standing or walking.

Swimming and cycling are the best exercises to keep you fit during rehabilitation. Both of these sports limit the amount of pressure on the injury

HAMSTRING MUSCLES

These are the structures most commonly damaged in the hamstrings.

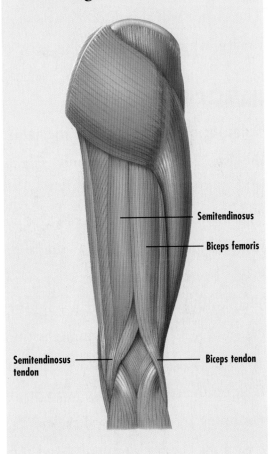

Semitendinosus

Biceps femoris

Semitendinosus tendon

Biceps tendon

while enabling you to keep the muscles in shape. Ease back into training with short, undemanding runs, and see if the pain returns. If it does, extend the period of convalescence or go to see a doctor.

In acute cases of shin splints, you may need a visit to the doctor's, anyway. Professional treatments can include **ultrasound** massage and physical therapy. The doctor will also discover whether you have a more serious **stress fracture** in the leg, which could require surgery, crutches, or a cast.

HAMSTRING INJURIES

Set at the back of each thigh, the hamstrings are a group of three muscles that flex the leg. They are commonly strained or ruptured by runners involved in sprinting, especially by explosive starts from the blocks and by fast accelerations. The injured person may feel a distinctive popping sensation at the moment of rupture, followed by pain at the back of the thigh and limited mobility in the knee. There may sometimes be swelling and even bruising behind the knee. Thankfully, most hamstring injuries are fully treatable by following the P.R.I.C.E., R.O.M., and strengthening sequence.

For the R.O.M. stage, use the following exercise:

1. Sit on the edge of a table, with one leg over the edge of the table and the other running straight along the side.

2. Keeping the back straight, bend forward from the waist over the outstretched leg until you feel a stretch in the back of the thigh and hamstrings. Hold for fifteen to twenty seconds, then release. Repeat the sequence five times.

3. Repeat for the other leg.

A good strengthening exercise is the hip extension:

1. Lie on the floor face down with the legs out straight behind you.

A rare event. Both Dwain Chambers (UK) and Mark Lewis Francis (UK) had to drop out of the 100 meters (110 yd) final in the Commonwealth Games because of injuries sustained during the sprint.

2. Lift one leg off the floor, keeping it straight, as far as your back muscles will allow. Hold the leg in this position for five seconds, then lower to the floor. Repeat three times.

3. Repeat for the other leg.

HIP INJURIES

Like knee injuries, hip injuries are of many different causes and types. Women seem to be slightly more prone to hip injuries than men, but all runners may experience painful or clicking hips from time to time. The symptoms depend on the type of injury. Ruptured muscles or **tendons** are expressed in sharp stabbing pains in the hip joint and a sudden feeling of weakness when you take a step. Alternatively, strained muscles or tendons produce aches in the hip during and after exercise. In all hip injuries, pain usually increases with movement and the whole joint area is tender to touch.

Hip injuries tend to occur when the lower limbs are placed under heavy stress. Running up hills and practicing sprint starts are typical causes. The treatment follows the P.R.I.C.E., R.O.M., and strengthening sequence, though hip injuries tend to respond better to heat treatments than ice treatments.

There are a huge range of R.O.M. and strengthening techniques for hip injuries. To strengthen the hip, try the following exercises:

1. Lie on your uninjured side, with your lower leg bent at a right angle for stability, and the top leg straight.
2. Slowly lift your top leg straight up to your side, until you can lift it no further.
   Hold it in the raised position for five seconds, then lower it slowly to the floor.
3. Repeat fifteen times.

1. Lie on your injured side. Place your top leg behind the leg on the floor.
2. Slowly raise the lower leg about 6 in. (15 cm.) off the floor. Hold for five seconds, then lower.
3. Repeat fifteen times.

SPRAINED ANKLES

Sprained ankles are another common runner's injury. The sprain is usually caused by a fall or trip, in which the ankle is put through an unnatural range of movement.

ANKLE TENDONS

These are the structures most commonly damaged in the ankle.

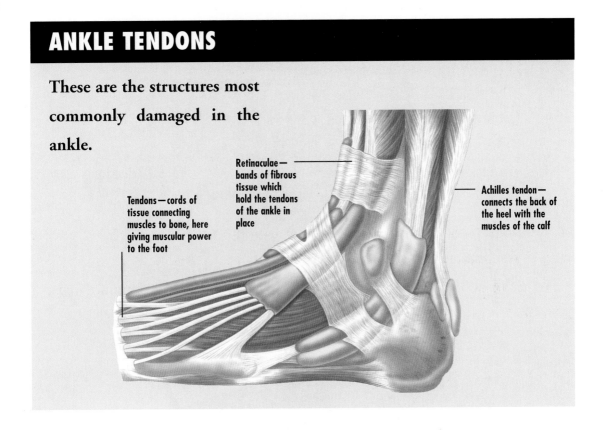

Retinaculae— bands of fibrous tissue which hold the tendons of the ankle in place

Tendons—cords of tissue connecting muscles to bone, here giving muscular power to the foot

Achilles tendon— connects the back of the heel with the muscles of the calf

A sprained ankle is characterized by a painful swollen ankle joint; worsening pain with movement or pressure on the joint; and, often, bruising and swelling. A practical strengthening exercise is the heel raise:

1. Stand up straight with your feet close together.
2. Slowly raise yourself on your toes as high as you can, then slowly lower yourself to the floor.
3. Repeat fifteen times.

For this exercise, you may find it necessary to steady yourself against a wall. Repeat these exercises daily until you have pain-free movement.

Careers in Track Events

The governing body for track and field, long-distance running, and racewalking in the United States is U.S.A. Track and Field. Its mission is, among other things, to promote running at amateur and professional levels throughout the United States.

Competitions for runners are held throughout the United States at local, regional, and national levels. At the most basic level, you can usually compete for running titles within your own school or in inter-school competitions. Advancing higher means competing in U.S.A. Track and Field events for Junior and Youth competitors. To compete in USATF events, you must first become a USATF member. It is also useful to train in a USATF club so that you learn the approved rules and regulations you will face in events. Finding a club near you and applying for membership can be done online, through the USATF website at www.usatf.org.

USATF has two major types of competition each year for young amateurs. These are the "Junior" program and "Youth" program events, which give young athletes the chance to compete at the highest standards. Each year, there are Youth and Junior category Track and Field championships. The distinctive feature of the Youth championships is that they are open to any athlete who fits within the age

Anthuan Maybank (U.S.A.) races in the men's 4 x 400 meters (440 yd) relay in the Atlanta Olympic Games, 1996. Maybank was part of the U.S. relay team which secured first place just ahead of the United Kingdom.

For most athletes it takes ten years of training to rise to professional level, beginning at high school.

ranges and is a USATF member. The USATF publishes a list of the times, distances, and heights required to win an event. Thousands of young people attend the competition, and it is an invaluable way to gain experience.

QUALIFYING FOR JUNIORS

Junior Championship events have stricter entry codes. Entrants must meet qualifying standards in their event in order to enter. For example, in the 2003 Junior Outdoor Track and Field Championships, entrants in the 100 meters had to meet a qualifying standard of 10.64 seconds for men and 11.94 seconds for women. The qualifying standards are verified at local and regional USATF competitions prior to the championships, and the entry code is strict.

Athletes who are 0.1 percent below the qualifying standard in running events can register for the competition, but are accepted into the championships only if there are not enough competitors, or if someone drops out.

The most prestigious event in the young field athlete's calendar is the National Junior Olympic Championships. This is part of the National Junior Olympic program, which USATF describes as "a progressional series of meets consisting of Preliminary, Association, Regional, and National meets." Athletes have to work their way up through the various stages by meeting the qualifying standards in each level of event; they cannot skip a stage. The National Junior Olympic Championships are the highest stage of this process. Athletes who finish in the top three of each regional meet in their respective events can go on to the championships.

Here, American athlete Maurice Greene leads on the final stretch in the 4 x 100 meters (110 yd) relay race at the 2000 Olympic Games in Sydney, Australia.

ELITE COMPETITORS

Becoming a member of the U.S. National Track-and-Field Team is similar to advancing up the Junior ladder. You have to be eighteen or older. If you meet the qualifying standards during trials you may take a place on the national team.

As you would expect, the qualifying standards for national and international level performance are the highest possible. For example, just to get into the U.S. Olympic Track and Field Trials, you might have to demonstrate a 100 meters time of 10.07 seconds for men and 11.15 seconds for women, or a 1,500 meters time of 3 minutes 39

Marion Jones waves to the crowds after winning the gold medal for the 100 meters (110 yd) in the World championship in Seville, Spain, in 1999.

seconds for men or 4 minutes 1 second for women—all times based on 2003 qualifying standards. Competitors who finish in the top two of the U.S.A. Indoor Track and Field Championships have the opportunity to compete in the **IAAF** World Indoor Track and Field Championships.

Dedicated athletes might base their choice of a university on the quality of its athletic facilities. Good coaching is available throughout the United States at the local or regional level. Certain universities, however, have traditions of excellence that attract athletes worldwide. Examples include Louisiana State University, the University of California at Los Angeles, and the University of Texas.

DAN O'BRIEN

Dan O'Brien is a world-class U.S. athlete who has overcome injury on many occasions. As a decathlon athlete, he established a world record in 1992, won an Olympic gold medal in 1996, and has been World Champion three times and National Champion five times. He has also battled through many injuries. In 1988, he was unable to complete the Olympic trials after he injured his leg in the long jump, but he returned to national competitions the very next year.

By 1991, he had become a World Championships gold medalist. In 1997, he suffered further injury—a stress fracture in his right leg. This prevented him from competing that year, but the next year he won a gold medal at the Goodwill Games. Since 2000, further injuries have kept Dan out of competitions, but at the time of this writing, he plans to return to the decathlon as soon as possible.

Dan O'Brien, world champion decathlon athlete. He ascribes success in sport and in life to "discipline and determination," and also believes we must accept the occasional defeat.

Glossary

Abdominals: The muscles concentrated in the abdomen, from the center of the chest to the groin.

Achilles tendon: A prominent tendon at the back of the heel, which joins the heel with the lower-leg muscles.

Femur: The thigh bone.

Flexor: A muscle that bends a limb or moves a joint.

Freeweights: Weight-training equipment consisting simply of a bar onto which weights are placed.

Gluteus maximus: A large muscle in the buttocks, which assists in moving the thigh.

Hamstrings: The group of three muscles set at the back of the thigh, which are used to flex the leg.

IAAF: International Association of Athletics Federations, a major governing body of international athletics.

Ligament: A short band of tough body tissue, which connects bones or holds together joints.

Midsole: The cushion foam in the sole of a sports shoe.

Overpronation: A tendency for the arch of the foot to collapse inward to an excessive degree when walking.

Physiology: The branch of science dealing with the normal function of human bodies.

Physical therapy: The treatment of an injury or illness using physical techniques such as massage and stretching, rather than medicines or surgery.

P.M.A.: Abbreviation for Positive Mental Attitude.

P.R.I.C.E.: An acronym for the common method of treating non-serious sprains and strains—Protection, Rest, Ice, Compression, Elevation.

Pronation: The way the arch of the foot rolls inward slightly as it absorbs the pressure of a step.

Quadriceps: A large four-part muscle on the front of the thigh, which is used to extend the leg.

R.O.M.: Abbreviation for Range of Motion, which may describe exercises designed to restore full flexibility to a damaged joint or muscle.

Sartorius muscles: A muscle running at an angle from the hip bone across the thigh to the knee.

Star jumps: An exercise in which the athlete jumps in and out of an "X" shape made with the arms and legs.

Stress fracture: A crack in a bone resulting from repetitive strain.

Supination: A tendency for the arch of the foot to roll outward to an excessive degree when stepping.

Tendon: A cord of body tissue connecting a muscle to a bone.

Tibia: A large bone between the knee and the ankle.

Ultrasound: Sound waves that are outside the range of human hearing. Physical therapists sometimes use ultrasound machines to treat damaged muscles by sending the sound waves vibrating through the injured area.

Underpronation: Little or no inward roll of the foot when walking.

Upper: The part of a shoe which surrounds the top and sides of your foot.

Visualization: A technique for improving sports performance by training in the imagination.

Further Information

USEFUL WEB SITES

International Association of Athletics Federations: www.iaaf.org

For news and events on track and field in the U.S., try:

www.runnersworld.com

www.track-and-field.net

U.S.A. Track and Field: www.usatf.org

The Web sites listed on this page were active at the time of publication. The publisher is not responsible for Web sites that have changed their address or discontinued operation since the date of publication. The publisher will review and update the Web sites upon each reprint.

FURTHER READING

Carr, Gerland. *Fundamentals of Track and Field.* Champaign, Illinois: Human Kinetics, 2000.

Ellis, Joe and Joe Henderson. *Running Injury-Free: How to Prevent, Treat and Recover from Dozens of Painful Problems.* Emmaus, Pennsylvania: Rodale Press, 1994.

Faigenbaum, Avery and Wayne Westcott. *Strength and Power Training for Young Athletes.* Champaign, Illinois: Human Kinetics, 2000.

Guthrie, Mark. *Coaching Track and Field Successfully.* Champaign, Illinois: Human Kinetics, 2003.

Peterson, Lars and Per Renström. *Sports Injuries.* London: Martin Dunitz, 2001.

Rodgers, Joseph L. *USA Track and Field Coaching Manual.* Champaign, Illinois: Human Kinetics, 1999.

THE AUTHOR

Dr. Chris McNab is a writer and editor specializing in sports, survival, and other human-performance topics. He has written more than twenty-five books, and recent publications include *Survival First Aid, Martial Arts for People with Disabilities, Living Off the Land*, and *How to Pass the SAS Selection Course*. Chris lives in South Wales, U.K.

THE CONSULTANTS

Susan Saliba, Ph.D., is a senior associate athletic trainer and a clinical instructor at the University of Virginia in Charlottesville, Virginia. A certified athletic trainer and licensed physical therapist, Dr. Saliba provides sports medicine care, including prevention, treatment, and rehabilitation for the varsity athletes at the University. Dr. Saliba holds dual appointments as an Assistant Professor in the Curry School of Education and the Department of Orthopaedic Surgery. She is a member of the National Athletic Trainers' Association's Educational Executive Committee and its Clinical Education Committee.

Eric Small, M.D., a Harvard-trained sports medicine physician, is a nationally recognized expert in the field of sports injuries, nutritional supplements, and weight management programs. He is author of *Kids & Sports* (2002) and is Assistant Clinical Professor of Pediatrics, Orthopedics, and Rehabilitation Medicine at Mount Sinai School of Medicine in New York. He is also Director of the Sports Medicine Center for Young Athletes at Blythedale Children's Hospital in Valhalla, New York. Dr. Small has served on the American Academy of Pediatrics Committee on Sports Medicine for the past six years, where he develops national policy regarding children's medical issues and sports.

Index